Leadership Through the Lens of the 12 Step

Cover design and interior design by José Pepito Jr.

Editing by D. Arthur

First edition – September, 2020

Visit our website at: www.ShallowhornConsulting.com

CONTENTS

INTRODUCTION

The 11th Step of Alcoholics Anonymous, Narcotics Anonymous, and all of the 12 Step programs, states: "Our public relations policy is based on attraction rather than promotion; we need always maintain personal anonymity at the level of press, radio, and films." This policy ensures that no one person is seen as a spokesperson or reflection of these programs.

That said, my 32-plus year experience as a member of NA is, in major part, my inspiration for writing this manual. And while I've adapted the 12 Steps, I have to acknowledge my predecessors who had the vision of creating a simple, yet impactful set of principles that have served to shape the lives of millions of people since the founding of AA in 1935.

In the same manner, as previously stated, I am but one of the many individuals who has walked the path of recovery. And for that community, I am eternally grateful.

MY STORY

In the years between 1980 and 1988, my life was controlled by drugs. This, combined with co-occurring bipolar disorder, made life a living hell. I endured many psychiatric hospitalizations for my condition, including at the Buffalo Psychiatric Center, a long-term facility for those who live with severe mental illness.

I was also in outpatient counseling at Horizon Health Services throughout this period. Having cycled through several counselors, I was eventually matched with Dick Heffron, a post-Vietnam era veteran who'd spend our sessions smoking Marlboros and drinking coffee from a thermos. But I liked Dick. I finally had found someone I could connect with.

On January 13, 1988, Dick presented me with a set of options. On that fateful day, he knew I wasn't "clean." He also recognized my pattern—using, hospitalization, and abstinence—that had repeated itself for the previous seven years. With this knowledge he said, "You have three choices: go to rehab, go to a Narcotics Anonymous meeting, or end up back in the hospital."

It didn't take me long to acknowledge that I didn't want to go to rehab for fear of telling my boss I had a drug problem. I also didn't want to be back in the psych hospital again. So, I chose the NA route.

Two days later, coincidentally Dr. Martin Luther King Jr.'s birthday ("Free at last! Free at last! Thank God almighty, I'm free at last!"), I attended my first NA meeting. Despite being under the influence when I walked through the doors of the church hall, I left with a measure of hope. Hope that maybe, just maybe, I could stop using.

That was the beginning of my journey in recovery. One of my first actions was to get a sponsor, a key concept of recovery in relation to leadership. I received a "Basic Text," the book that serves as one of the foundational pieces of literature in the NA program. The Basic Text contains various chapters that help the recovering addict learn a new way of life. One of these chapters details the 12 Steps – a set of guiding principles for recovery programs that provides practical guidance on how to apply these steps to one's life. As with all other 12 Step related programs, the steps were written by people in recovery. But this is what, I believe makes them so valuable.

As we say in the program, "The therapeutic value of one addict helping another is without parallel."

From my first days in NA and through until today, I've tried to "work" the steps to the best of my availability by going to meetings, working with a sponsor, and maintaining deep abiding relationships, some lasting decades.

NA saved me from a life of dereliction and despair. I have learned a new way to live and take the spiritual principles taught in the program to apply them to my daily affairs. I have also learned that, while I continue to put into action these principles, I will never be perfect. This humility in my life has helped me remain teachable. I recognize that regardless of my role in whatever part of my life, I will always have room to grow.

WHAT ARE THE 12 STEPS?

The 12 Steps serve several purposes. They are a path to self-discovery. They help to renew and/or foster relationships with others and with a "Higher Power.' They also emphasize the importance of service.

The primary purpose of the 12 Steps, as described in program literature, is abstinence from specific maladaptive behaviors, such as excessive drinking, drug use, gambling, sex, etc. The rules were originally written to support Alcoholics Anonymous and have been adapted to support many 12 Step programs.

The 12 Steps themselves, however, provide far more than the simple promotion of abstinence from substance use or negative behaviors. In fact, only Step One references the concept of powerlessness over such behaviors. The remaining eleven are designed to ultimately help the individual become the best version of who they can be.

For me, my journey in recovery has enabled me to gain valuable insight into myself, my thoughts, my words, and my deeds. First and foremost, I have learned that while I am constantly seeking ways to grow, I will never achieve perfection. This idea of self-acceptance is an extremely important aspect of the 12 Steps. It is strongly correlated to the principle of humility, which will be further explained later in Step Seven.

As far as leadership is concerned, I have had countless opportunities to learn from both my mistakes and my successes. Early on, this learning centered on things such as proper task delegation and setting appropriate boundaries. As I progressed in my career, this learning evolved to understand the value of more profound elements, including emotional intelligence and servant leadership.

HISTORY OF THE 12 STEPS

Alcoholics Anonymous was founded in June, 1935 by Bill W. and Dr. Bob S. Bill was a stockbroker who had made several attempts to get sober with limited success. He was on a business trip in Akron, Ohio and was interested in speaking with another person who shared his same affliction. He was introduced to Dr. Bob and the two immediately connected.

Bill and Dr. Bob had each been in contact with the Oxford Group, a mostly nonalcoholic fellowship that emphasized universal spiritual values in daily living. After their immediate connection, they quickly had a mutual desire to share a newfound approach to addressing alcoholism. They did so, at first, by working with individuals at Akron's City Hospital where they were able to help one individual achieve sobriety.

From there the program grew, first in New York City and then in Cleveland. It took over four years to produce 100 sober alcoholics in these three groups. In 1939, the Fellowship produced its first textbook, Alcoholics Anonymous, written by Bill. It included the underlying philosophy of the program, including the Twelve Steps.

These simple, yet powerful, actions have been the guiding resource for literally millions of people who have been members of AA and all of the other 12 Step fellowships that have followed. Many, myself included, have stated that the 12 Steps have saved our lives. The power found in the 12 Steps lies in the underlying spiritual principles that serve as their foundation. One common misunderstanding about the 12 Steps is the idea that you must believe in God to apply them to your life. While they, as previously stated, center around spiritual principles, this concept of what a "Higher Power" consists of is entirely up to the individual and is not dogmatic in nature. In fact, there are some members who consider themselves atheists. These individuals' belief in a Power greater than themselves may be the group or nature, for instance. Anything that helps the person achieve their goal of abstinence and is outside of the individual can be utilized.

SPIRITUAL VS. LEADERSHIP PRINCIPLES

The objective behind this book is to examine yourself and the work you do, thereby enabling you to become the best leader you can be. This can only be accomplished through the ability to look at yourself from every angle. It is recommended that you work with a trusted person, such as a coach, who is familiar with your work. This person can help you maintain the objectivity necessary to be effective in the process.

Yes, the 12 Steps of the various Anonymous programs have spiritual principles as a foundation. But when you look at them more closely, what you will see is that they address many of the characteristics necessary for successful leadership. Honesty, for instance, is an integral part of both 12 Steps and good leadership. Without it, there is no basis for the decisions you will make.

This correlation is found in each of the 12 Steps. This book illuminates how these principles can be seen as a blueprint to work from. These ideas may seem like common sense, but oftentimes when looking at these concepts a different "spin" can serve to stimulate new ideas.

HOW TO USE THIS WORKBOOK

In each section, I will provide some questions for reflection. These questions also provide a framework for conversations with your coach, or other accountability partner. The intent behind working with someone on these exercises is to help you gain valuable, objective feedback on what you uncover and any potential issues that need to be resolved.

Secondly, I would encourage you to take your time. This is not work that is meant to be rushed through. By using a thoughtful approach, you will gain more insight into yourself and develop the knowledge to help you become a better leader.

Finally, rigorous self-honesty is necessary in this process of introspection. It is vital that you be willing to look at yourself in a manner that is centered around self-acceptance and allows room for growth. Without this approach, you may not be able to fully address your areas in need of improvement while still acknowledging your strengths.

So, let's begin!

THE 12-STEPS

One consideration must be emphasized. There is a saying we have in NA, "Take what you need and leave the rest behind." Some of the themes you read here may not resonate with you and that's okay. Resist the urge to diminish their power. As you will see, these guiding questions serve to help you to uncover who you are, not only as a leader but also as a person. It's all about discovering your potential. I believe that everyone, regardless of their standing, can develop their skills and become more effective.

We admitted that we were powerless over others, that our lives had become unmanageable.

Honesty is the central principle of Step One. It is important to be truthful with yourself and examine your thoughts, actions, and motivations. This requires rigorous self-examination while allowing for the understanding that imperfection is expected and there is always room for improvement.

Honesty is essential to leadership. A common buzz word we hear these days is "transparency." What does transparency really mean? When you are transparent, you sometimes have to admit you were wrong. More specifically, in the case of this step, you have to admit that life has become unmanageable in one form or another due to your inability to control another person's actions.

In one role in my career, I was faced with a particularly challenging situation. One of my staff was taking liberties and pushing the limits when it came time to taking breaks. While I attempted to address this behavior, I was met with considerable resistance and a sense of entitlement from that staff member, who happened to be heavily involved with our organization's union. I was extremely frustrated with their lack of respect and professionalism. In the end, I simply threw up my hands and essentially stopped fighting.

This was many years ago and if it were to happen again, I'd certainly handle things differently. I could have approached the situation in a manner that would not have been as confrontational and instead utilized skills, like engagement, to pursue a less adversarial approach to addressing the behavior.

Hope is another principle found in Step One. How does hope relate to leadership? First, hope is a necessary mindset you must have, especially in today's business climate. Pressures on leaders are universal, whether you are a CEO, Executive Director, or mid-level manager. A measure of hope is necessary to have the confidence you need to deal with these uncertain times.

In the world of work, nothing is guaranteed. With this understanding, hope can provide the sense that things can, and will, get better when you are faced with adversity. I live by this axiom. Whether I am facing audits, accreditation reviews, or the seemingly ever-shrinking funds in the nonprofit sector, I have to have hope.

I often had to rely on a sense of hope during my tenure working in higher education at Daemen College, a small private institution located outside of Buffalo. I served as Associate Director of Graduate Admissions. At that time, Daemen had to compete against 27 other colleges in the Western New York region. This posed a considerable challenge to meeting our enrollment numbers. Anytime a student submitted a tuition deposit was a cause for celebration. In the four years I worked there, having hope was necessary. Mind you, there was a lot of work involved in meeting our targets but in the end, it started with hope.

Step One Reflection Questions – Understanding Powerlessness:

- The concept of "powerlessness" is a central tenant of Step One. This comes into play when we are dealing with others' behaviors, for better or worse. When have you had this experience and how did you handle it?

- One aspect of recovery is living "life on life's terms." How do you deal with the decisions you make? Do you dig in your heels, or do you roll with the punches?

- When have you felt that you've lost control over a situation? How did that make you feel?

- Do you find yourself trying to "fill the void" in your life by overworking? Do you practice healthy boundaries between your work and personal life?

- Self-centeredness can contribute to the feeling of "my way or the highway." Do you ever find yourself in this mode of thinking? If so, how can you change this belief system?

- Finally, in terms of powerlessness, consider what it takes to accept that, in the end, you may not have as much power as you think you do, over others or situations. Have you come to accept this as a reality? If so, what helped you to reach this conclusion?

STEP TWO

We came to believe that a Power greater than ourselves could restore us to sanity.

Step Two is a process that may not be accomplished immediately. You may "come to believe" many times thereby reinforcing the experiences you've had which can serve as a foundation to your leadership style.

This step, as written here, is the same as it was originally written. But this Power doesn't have to be spiritual in nature, although it can be. As far as leadership is concerned, this Power can be anything—your team, your Board, a coach, or maybe a trusted colleague.

The principle of open-mindedness is key to Step Two. Each time you consider different options or approaches to a problem, you have the opportunity to learn from your team or those with whom your consult. Sometimes this relinquishment of control is necessary to allow the process to unfold. By "letting go," it's possible to achieve your desired goal or goals without forcing the situation.

Many times, when facing a dilemma in your work you may feel like you've lost control over a situation or that there is an unsolvable problem. By opening yourself up to the fact that other people may have ideas worth exploring, you can develop a true sense that, through this admission, you don't have all the answers. And that it's okay to not have all the answers. No one ever does.

In 2018, I participated in the Health Leadership Fellows Program, an initiative of the Health Foundation of Western and Central New York. This 18-month residency program focused on developing leadership skills of nonprofit leaders through a variety of activities, including retreats led by assessment and communication, and group work that was developed by team coaches. Each individual also received 4 hours of professional coaching. It was both incredibly humbling and eye-opening.

The key feature of this program is a capstone project developed by group members and guided by the team coach. Our group was diverse, including two nonprofit Executive Directors, a Chief Financial Officer, a manager who oversaw a WIC program, a County Deputy Commissioner, and me.

When faced with the prospect of developing our project, we went through Bruce Tuckman's traditional "storming, norming, and performing" process. This process centers the way that teams can learn to work together effectively. The storming phase is when individuals in the group work through conflicts, such as differing working styles or dealing with individuals who challenge authority. The norming stage is when the team begins to "gel" and people resolve their differences. The performing period is when the true work begins, leading to the achievement of the team's goals. It was quite remarkable that we went from essentially a blank slate to a project that demonstrated the value of supported decision making as an alternative to guardianship for older adults.

I learned that, it's true what we say in the NA program, "what I can't do alone, we can do together." If it had been left up to any one of us individually, I'm certain that coming up with this idea would have been virtually impossible. But through our collective effort, we were able to accomplish something that was both innovative and held value.

The ability to creatively brainstorm as a team is essential for today's world of work. True leaders use these opportunities to recognize that.

Step Two Reflection Questions – Keeping an Open Mind:

- Insanity has been described as "making the same mistakes over and over again, expecting different results." Have you ever found yourself in this pattern of thinking? Describe it as well as what, if anything, you were able to do to center yourself and get back on track.

- Have you ever made a decision without regard for the wellbeing of yourself or others? Describe this experience.

- Describe a time when you needed help from others to provide clarity on a project you were overseeing.

- In respect to a "Power greater" than oneself, who do you lean on for advice on decisions you are making? Your Board, co-workers, a coach, or mentor? If you prefer to go it alone, who can you try to lean on more in the future?

STEP THREE

We made a decision to turn our will and our lives over to the care of a Power greater than ourselves.

Willingness is the main principle found in Step 3. Once you come understand the need for a Power greater than yourself, you then need to become willing to allow that Power to help guide you. At this point, you've admitted that there are things out of your control and that you need help from something, or someone, greater than yourself.

As this step also implies, it's about making a decision and turning your life over to the care of your interpretation of a Power greater than yourself. It is important to state here that the term "Power" can represent whatever you want it to be. Many do not ascribe to spirituality, and that's okay. What I am talking about here is approaching leadership from the perspective of someone who can tackle any number of problems through a clear decision-making process based on the best available information. I am also talking about having the faith that things will be able to be resolved, despite how challenging they may be.

Whereas in Step Two, it was about "coming to believe," Step Three has to do with making a decision—one that is not based on acting out of self-will. This aspect of leadership is clear. When a leader operates from the mindset of "my way or the highway," it can be a recipe for failure. This line of thinking can be seen as egotistical and autocratic. As a result, those in an organization led by this type of leader can have a wide range of emotion in response, including anger, frustration, and even despair.

Ultimately, you will need to be the decision maker. The buck stops with you. I've worked with several grants that have required me to make decisions with a team. In my tenure at the organizations I've worked at, it has been interesting to observe the different leadership styles of the executives. Some were more hands-on, whereas others were more laissez-faire, delegating oversight to others. What I've learned is that the key to effective leadership, in such cases, is to allow your team members to contribute in a meaningful way thereby creating a true collaborative atmosphere.

One of my most memorable experiences with this was when I worked simultaneously at the Mental Health Advocates of Western New York and Compeer Buffalo. The MHA was working on a statewide Medicaid redesign program called DSRIP (Delivery System Reform Incentive Program). This was a massive 5-year federally funded initiative meant to reduce costs to New York State by addressing key indicators that would reduce avoidable hospital use by those receiving Medicaid by 25% in this 5-year period.

The DSRIP program was administered by Performance Provider Systems (PPS). These regional hospital-based providers were responsible for contracting with both large medical-based centers as well as health and social service providers. Each PPS was required to choose ten projects that were prescribed by the New York State Medicaid Redesign Team (MRT).

The MHA was contracted to work with the two PPSs in Western New York, Millennium Collaborative Care and Community Partners of WNY. We were tasked to work on Project 4.a.i., to promote mental, emotional and behavioral health (MEB) well-being in communities.

This was a massive undertaking for a relatively small nonprofit. In our agreements with Millennium and Community Partners, we actively worked to achieve outcomes while also subcontracting with other community-based organizations to meet our goals.

The Executive Director of the MHA, at the time, was Ken Houseknecht. I worked directly with Ken on the implementation of the project. This was a very pivotal time in my growth as a professional. I had to produce at a high level while juggling multiple responsibilities, including overseeing a federal grant for Mental Health First Aid (MHFA). As a middle manager I found it necessary to both meet the expectations of Ken, as well as Michele Brown, Executive Director of Compeer, and the individuals on the MHFA instructor team.

There were times when I had to follow the direction of both Ken and Michele, which posed its own challenges. I also had to coordinate the MHFA program. Between DSRIP, MHFA, and the other projects at the MHA and Compeer, I became adept at walking the line between being managed and being a manager.

I also learned the value of collaboration and decision making. Each of these projects required proper leadership to achieve their objectives. I was an integral part of the leadership team for DSRIP on top of heading up MHFA. I was able to observe the different leadership styles of Ken and Michele while continuing to develop my own. Ken's style was more outcome-focused and centered on a "bottom line approach" whereas Michele's style was more humanistic in nature, and guided by a sense of providing services.

I often found myself in the middle of these two people who cared deeply about those living with mental health challenges and I had to deftly serve as an intermediary between them. This in itself posed its own challenges. As the old saying goes, "A servant cannot serve two masters." What I learned, however, was how to use tact and diplomacy at all times and to never undercut either one of them or manipulate them in any way, pitting one against the other.

Step Three is an action step. When you find yourself stuck, this can be an opportunity to seek the guidance of others from your team. By doing so, you can unlock the answers to what may, at first, have seemed to be an impossible problem.

Step Three Reflection Questions – The Process of Becoming Willing:

- What is your decision-making process? Do you tend to operate by formula or are you more of a spontaneous decision maker? Do you ever find yourself second-guessing your decisions?

- Making a decision is based on action. Describe a time when you took action that involved the welfare of your staff/employees or colleagues. What did you take into consideration when you made this decision?

- How do you use others as a "sounding board" for decisions you make?

- Another aspect of this step is "will." Do you ever find yourself operating out of self-will, and if so, how does it affect your business relationships?

- Have you ever been dishonest in your dealings with others or in the decisions you've made? If so, what have you learned through this experience? Were these actions worth the potential risks?

- Communication is an integral part of the work we do. How would you describe your communication style? How does this impact your leadership in your organization?

- Another essential piece to this step is turning your will over "to the care of" a Power greater than yourself. Considering that collectively your organization is a Power greater than yourself, as an individual, do you trust that you can rely on your team to support you? Describe a time when you had to let go and trust this Power greater than yourself at work.

We made a searching and fearless moral inventory of ourselves.

Step Four requires rigorous self-honesty. By looking at ourselves in a forthright manner, we can truly learn where we need to grow. This can be a difficult and challenging process. In my 28 years as a professional, I've had countless opportunities to examine myself through a variety of means: involvement with my 12-Step program, professional therapy, professional assessments, colleagues, supervisors, mentors, and coaches. It has been through these associations that I have gained insight into myself, not only professionally but as a human being. It hasn't always been easy and there have been many times I would have liked to change my past actions. However, it has been through these experiences that I've been able to change, I believe, for the better.

At the beginning of the Health Leadership Fellows Program we were required to complete three assessments: the MBTI, FIRO-B and a 360 assessment. Each of these assessments provided me with a different look at myself. The Myers-Briggs assessment provided me with an indication of my personality type, the FIRO-B measured how I feel when it comes to inclusion, control, and affection/openness as well as the ability to get feedback from people in a group. The 360 assessment gave me a better understanding of the way I operated at work from the perspective of my two supervisors at the time, peers, and individuals who had reported to me.

The experience was very humbling. These assessments revealed my strengths as well as the areas in which I needed improvement. But ultimately, they were invaluable in terms of the insights they provided me about the various aspects of my leadership style.

The principle associated with Step Four is faith. You're probably asking yourself, "What does faith have to do with leadership?" You may not even ascribe to spiritual beliefs. Faith, in this context, represents the ability to look at yourself and have a deep understanding of where you are as an individual. As stated previously, this ability requires rigorous honesty and a deep resolve to be unflinching in your examination of yourself from all angles.

In Step Four, you are looking for your assets as well as your liabilities. For many, myself included, it's easy to get stuck on just those areas that need improvement. Don't forget to acknowledge the things you do well. Chances are there are more of these than the opposite.

When you work through the following guiding questions, don't hold back. Remember, this is for you to learn about yourself.

Step Four Reflection Questions – Practicing Self-Honestly:

- You may have a sense of fear regarding approaching this step. What do you believe this fear stems from? Will it keep you from being rigorously honest with yourself?

- What kind of self-assessment tools do you use/have you used in the past? What insights have you learned from them?

- How do you go about reconciling any errors in judgment you may have made in your work? Is it difficult to admit that you've been wrong?

- This step asks you to make a searching and fearless *moral* inventory of yourself. How do you navigate your business world? Do you follow certain principles and values? What are they?

- Step Four also looks at our assets. What leadership qualities do you feel are your strengths? When/how have you used those strengths?

- Our relationships at work, in many ways, define who we are. How would you describe your work relationships? Are they mutually beneficial, or one-sided?

- What goals are you still trying to achieve? What process do you utilize to track and strive toward these goals?

We admitted without reservation to ourselves and another human being the exact nature of our wrongs.

This step is more than recitation. It is much more than simply reading what you've written in Step Four. It entails being willing to be courageous, which is the principle of this step. This courage lies in the ability to trust someone enough to be completely open and vulnerable. This can be very difficult for you, especially if you are in an executive position that yields a limited circle of confidants. But most of us have at least one person with whom we can discuss our innermost challenges. You may have a coach or mentor who you've spoken to in the past and who is willing to hold your conversations in confidence.

When examining this step, it is also important to consider, once again, the importance of self-honesty, otherwise it is impossible to be truthful with others. It is also important to understand that we are all a work-in-progress and that even the best of leaders can recognize that there is always room for growth. In the end, when you take the time to share your challenges—and successes—with others, you can find great perspective on things you may not have previously considered.

During my tenure in higher education, I worked as the Associate Director of Admissions at Daemen College. Early on my friend Joe Pagano was hired as Coordinator of Transfer Student Admissions. Joe and I had a mutual interest in running. I had established a habit of running during my lunch hour and Joe started to join me. These were not high intensity runs, more like stress busters. It was during these times that Joe and I would talk about our challenges and successes at work. There were also many times I'd confide in Joe. I would speak with him about things that I wouldn't share with other staff.

I felt I could speak with Joe because we had both a sense of mutual respect as well as trust. I believed that what I shared with Joe would not be mentioned to anyone else, and vice-versa. Many times, these relationships are reciprocal. Especially when there is a shared experience. For me, these talks with Joe were a vital part of me being able to navigate the often-difficult waters of enrollment management. Sometimes all I needed was for Joe to listen and that was enough. Oftentimes, just having someone be present is enough. There are also times when feedback is necessary. Regardless of the situation, having someone available to serve as a source of trust and confidence is invaluable.

Step Five Reflection Questions – Finding Courage:

- Speak to a colleague about what you've uncovered in Step 4 and share what you've learned.

- Do you feel able to acknowledge when you may have been wrong in any way (decisions, interactions with others, etc.)?

- How will these admissions change how you work with others?

- Who will you choose to speak to about these matters?

- In what way(s) does practicing this step further your ability to lead?

- Have your relationships improved as a result of the work you've done here?

STEP SIX

We were entirely ready to remove all our defects of character.

Everyone has character defects, certainly some more than others, but we all have them. Taking this into consideration, it is important not to be overly alarmed by what you may see in yourself. Chances are, many others are dealing with the same thing. The important thing to remember is that the removal of these defects is a process and doesn't happen overnight.

There are two principles for Step Six: Self-acceptance and Perseverance. Self-acceptance is the principle that requires us to be willing to look at ourselves, warts and all. We are not perfect, nor will we ever be. Truth be told, I still, at times, struggle with self-acceptance. This, I believe, is a result of issues from childhood that served to create particular "hang-ups" (but this topic is for another book). Sometimes I experience the "I'm not good enough" syndrome, or the unrealistic expectation of perfection. I've come to realize that I'm okay just as I am, despite my occasional pangs of insecurity.

I've had many performance evaluations over the years. And while, typically, I've always done well, rarely if ever have I "exceeded expectations" in all ratings categories. Expecting to "exceed expectations" in all ratings is like expecting a perfect score on the GRE or GMAT. This isn't exactly realistic. If anything, it's a surefire way to set yourself up for disappointment. There is also the consideration that evaluations are subjective in nature and based on someone else's assessment of your performance on the job.

Despite the fact that you may not receive the stellar rating you think you deserve; you can use any evaluation as a learning experience. The purpose of these evaluations, after all, is to help you to grow as a professional.

Perseverance is associated with this step since we have to be willing to stick with the process of delving deeper into ourselves to acknowledge areas in our lives that need improvement. This is important in our work lives because once we can become willing to approach ourselves more objectively, we can truly begin to grow.

Performance evaluations can be great tools to learn from. Whenever I've gone through this process, I usually walk away with a few things that I learn about myself, including ways to get better at what I do. This requires a certain kind of diligence and willingness to take constructive criticism. Being able to develop into the best leader you can be takes time. No one begins their career in management with an overriding ability to get things right all the time.

I've seen improvement in my own performance over the years. One area of improvement in particular is in delegation. When I began my career as a manager, I would often try to complete a wide range of tasks that could be otherwise assigned to someone else. Part of this was the belief that if I didn't do it, the project wouldn't be done properly. This is an example of a major control issue. Over time, I've learned to let go and to allow others to take on certain responsibilities, thereby allowing me to make better use of my time. This allows the person taking on the delegated task an opportunity to grow as well.

It may take years to re-examine our behaviors and refine what we see to move forward in this journey of self-discovery. It's a marathon, not a sprint. The beauty is that we don't have to do it all at once. Sometimes it's easier to take a bite out of the elephant instead of trying to eat the whole thing at once.

Step Six Reflection Questions - Becoming the Leader You Are Intended to Be:

- When it comes to your potential areas for improvement, how willing are you to address these issues? Are you ready? Describe the process that got you to this point.

- How do you think your leadership skills will improve by working on this step?

- What defects have you uncovered?

- When you act out on these defects, how do they affect others?

- Are there any "defects" that you feel you may be unable to resolve?

- How have you, if ever, tried to address these issues? What level of success have you had? How long did it take to resolve these issues?

- What kind of leader can you envision yourself becoming as you grow?

We made a decision to address our faults and remove these shortcomings.

As previously mentioned in Step Six, we are not perfect. But this does not mean that we can't improve. It *IS* possible to address our imperfections and become a better version of ourselves. There are two primary principles associated with Step Seven: Patience and Humility. Patience derives from the necessity to understand that it takes time to become the person you were intended to be. Unfortunately, if you're like me, patience isn't always your strong suit. Additionally, you may have some more ingrained behaviors that may take more time to remove. That said, with the proper mindset, success is possible.

I've gone through a number of job changes over the years in the behavioral health and higher education arena. In several of these instances, I would get the itch to move on to something else. I was often asked about these moves, and frankly, I didn't always have a great response as to why I was moving around so frequently. In retrospect, however, I realize that this sense of impatience was grounded in my lack of true sense of direction for my career. It wasn't until I made a fateful decision to write an op-ed for the *Buffalo News* in which I outed myself as a person living with bipolar disorder that I discovered my passion was mental health advocacy.

Secondly, humility is an important principle because it's vital to embrace the concept of erasing any egotistical view of yourself and how you lead in order for this step to work. The concept of a servant leader, the main goal of the leader is to serve, comes to mind. When leading others, it is important to do so by example, and in collaboration with your team. How many times have you caught yourself with the belief that things had to be done your way?

Usually, when we are able to open our minds, it's possible to see a variety of options for decisions that need to be made. Why else are organizations typically built on some kind of shared leadership platform? Ultimately, the buck may stop with you. Even so, this does not diminish the significance of relying on a team approach to tackling work-related issues.

When I worked in higher education many years ago, I had a supervisor named Bill Hirsch. Bill was the Associate Vice-President for Enrollment Management at Buffalo State. I was the Coordinator of Transfer Student Services. He was the embodiment of humility. When working on projects with him, I always had the sense that we were working together, as opposed to me working for him. This partnership unlocked the opportunity to tackle challenging and complex issues. Transfer enrollment in higher ed has always been a challenge for institutions. Working with Bill not only helped to facilitate this process, but he also served as a mentor to me.

Step Seven Reflection Questions – Developing Humility Through Patience:

- Are you a patient person? Do you ever find yourself becoming impatient with your staff or colleagues? If so, how do you think you can remedy this?

- What about patience in your career path? Are you continuously looking for "the next thing" or are you able to be more patient, biding your time for the right opportunity?

- Discuss how the concept of humility corresponds to leadership and its importance in helping you to address your areas for improvement.

- When you consider working this step, based on what you've learned in Steps One through Six, what are some of the issues that you've observed and need to address?

- Have you ever been "called out" on a specific behavior or shortcoming? How did that make you feel? If you felt defensive in the moment, how would you approach things differently now? Did this prompt you to want to change that behavior or remove that shortcoming?

- Have you had any opportunities for growth in this particular area recently? If so, describe.

- As a result of working this step, what shortcomings have you been able to remove? What shortcomings are you still working to remove?

We made a list of all persons we had harmed and became willing to make amends to them all.

Up to this point you've focused on yourself. Now you are at a place where you are required to look at your professional relationships throughout your career. The first thing to understand is that this step is simply asking you to list the people you may have harmed. The term "harmed" can have many meanings. Sometimes it will refer to things you may have said to someone and in other instances, it can refer to concrete actions. At first thought, you may say to yourself, "Well, I've never harmed anyone!" What I would challenge you to do is to think deeply and look back over your career to examine the interactions you've had with others and ask yourself, "Has there been anything that I've done that has adversely affected this relationship?" or "What has been my part in this conflict?" You can always list the person for now and then revisit their inclusion on the list to determine if amends need to be offered to them.

The principle associated with this step is compassion. It is important to be compassionate because when looking back at potential harm, you need to practice empathy and consider how your actions affected the other person. When approaching a person this way, it's easier to get a sense of how they may have been impacted by what you said or did. Remember the adage, "Treat others as you, yourself would like to be treated."

I've worked in a variety of roles over the years. And yes, there have been cases where I've caused harm to someone else. I'm not proud to admit it, but that's the plain and simple truth. Of course, if I had it to do all over again, I would have certainly handled things differently. But this is the beauty of the 12 Steps. You can acknowledge that your imperfection and use the steps as a way to progress toward becoming the best leader you can be.

This step requires its own level of unflinching honesty as well. There are many leaders who, frankly, can be downright abusive, and that is not acceptable. In order to demonstrate that you can serve as a leader, you must not engage in any forms of abuse, harassment, or otherwise demeaning behavior. In New York State, where I'm from, for instance, nonprofit and for-profit organizations must hold annual sexual harassment training. Clear policies also need to be in place for staff to be able to safely address any workplace-related issues.

Step Eight Reflection Questions – Developing Compassion:

- Examine your professional relationships. Without thinking of how you'd address these individuals, list the people you've worked with who you may have treated improperly.

- It's important to think about ourselves in terms of the big picture when making amends. Sometimes we may have even harmed ourselves (lack of balance in your personal and professional life, for instance). In what ways have you harmed yourself?

- What things have you done or said that have caused harm?

- You may be reluctant to include certain individuals due to a resentment you may have against them. List these resentments and how they may contribute to your unwillingness to make amends to these people.

- What policies do you have in place at your organization, if any, to address issues around harassment? If you do not have these policies already, what policies can you institute moving forward?

We made direct amends to such people wherever possible, except when to do so would injure them or others.

The principle of this step is forgiveness. In your interactions with others throughout your career, you may have had occasions when you said or did something you regret. Now is the time to make things right. But first, you may want to enlist the help of a trusted advisor (coach, colleague, etc.) that may provide you with guidance on whether making amends to the individuals on your Step Eight list would pose a risk to the individual or to someone else. And as stated in Step Eight, you may be that person at risk. There could potentially be an instance where the amends process could put you at risk of losing your job. This is a matter of integrity, which is a fundamental element of leadership. Obviously, this is not a matter to be taken lightly. However, with the proper approach, relationships can be restored.

The key to this step is the knowledge that by making amends, you are relieving yourself of any guilt or shame connected to your actions. The ability to apologize for your actions can be an extremely liberating experience. Asking for forgiveness, not only from the other person, but ourselves as well, can be difficult. Self-forgiveness, in itself, can give one a sense of peace and comfort.

Also consider that you should not automatically expect an expression of forgiveness from the other person when you make your amends. Sometimes the hurt you caused is deep and has left an emotional scar.

In one particular instance, I was administering a program at an organization where I worked. We had hired an individual to be a subcontractor for this particular project. On one occasion, he called me at the very last minute to say that he was unable to make it, leaving me with the responsibility of delivering the program by myself. This, of course happens, so I was willing to allow for his late cancellation. Several weeks later, he did the same thing. I was furious. As far as I was concerned, he was not upholding the end of our agreement—albeit the agreement was not in writing, which was a mistake I realize, in retrospect.

Instead of setting up a meeting, or even calling him to discuss his absence, I texted him and ended up saying something to the effect of, "So, I guess our professional relationship is over." He texted back immediately, deflecting the blame by saying, "Is this how you handle this? And you consider yourself a mental health professional?" I was taken aback. Ultimately, after discussing the matter with my administration, we decided to no longer engage his services.

After reflection, I felt bad about how I handled the situation, regardless of the other person's role. I attempted to reach out with an apology via email however I received no reply.

I learned several valuable lessons through this experience: have a written contract when working with subcontractors, state clearly written deliverables and outcomes, and most importantly, when ending a business relationship, there are far more effective, and meaningful, ways to do so than by texting!

On the other hand, your expression of sincere apology may be met with a return of gratitude. Also, it may not be possible to make the amends due to a loss of contact or change in employment. That's okay. There are other ways to make indirect amends, such as not acting out on that behavior again. In NA there have been cases where people have written letters and burned them, or in the case of financial amends, made donations to agencies.

The action of making amends can be particularly daunting however the results can be transformational. It's amazing what amends can do to revitalize your spirit and reinvigorate relationships. Basically, it's more than just saying, "I'm sorry," when you break a window. You repair the window and vow not to break any more.

Step Nine Reflection Questions – Addressing Those You've Wronged:

- When considering the people with whom you'd like to make amends, it is recommended that you consult with someone who can affirm that the steps you plan to take will not be creating more damage. Who would this trusted person be?

- There may have been a time when both you and another person caused harm to each other. Are you willing to forgive them? Describe the situation and explain how you'd approach the individual to acknowledge your role in it.

- Have you accepted responsibility for the harm you may have caused to the other person, or yourself, in this situation? How do you intend to address that?

- Can you forgive yourself for your actions? What were they?

- Create an action plan for how you would address these issues with those on your list. Are there any themes you've discovered in your actions? How can you address a broader theme of behavior?

We continued to take personal inventory and when we were wrong promptly admitted it.

The purpose of this step is to be able to maintain our ability to regularly examine our behaviors and self-correct any that do not serve us, or those with whom we work, well. This can be done easily at the end of each workday by taking a moment to review what you experienced, whether it be your interactions with others or your deeds.

The core principle in this step is integrity. At the end of the day, you need to be able to look at yourself in the mirror and ask yourself, "Have I done anything that I wish I hadn't done?" It's a relatively simple question. However, ultimately only you know what you've done. Granted some of your regrettable actions may be in public view. But think about those actions that perhaps you wished you hadn't done that no one knows about. This requires you to, once again, be unabashedly honest with yourself, because after all, you have to live with every decision you make.

This is yet another time to be reminded that you are not perfect. Over the many years I've been in the workforce, I've done things I wish I hadn't. What I've come to learn, however, is that I need to maintain the highest level of integrity possible in order to know that my work is coming from a place of service and not self-driven motivation.

This is another time that you may need to check in with someone who may be able to provide a "reality check" to ascertain the degree of severity in the situation and what you may need to do to facilitate the appropriate action steps to remedy it.

Another primary consideration with this step is, *"when we were wrong promptly admitted it."* This, in itself, is important due to the fact that letting the admission of your potential wrongdoing go unresolved for too long may make you reluctant to eventually address it. You need to address any issues that may arise immediately in order to mitigate any further issues that may arise.

I've had occasions in my career, like you may have, where I "dropped the ball" on completing a task or following up on a particular issue. I learned very early that I benefitted by acknowledging my wrongdoing rather than thinking it would go unnoticed or could simply be wished away. This is where the principle of integrity comes in. In the majority of cases, when you recognize that you haven't done what was expected at the time and admit it, you're not met with scorn.

This is something leaders should recognize as well. When you have a subordinate come to you to admit that they missed a deadline or did not meet an expectation, recognize the great deal of courage it likely took to admit their error instead of immediately going into a rage and criticizing the person for failing to complete the task.

Do not be dismayed by wrongdoings. There are usually opportunities to correct things you regret that you've done. It all comes down to daily practice and taking the time for self-reflection.

Step Ten Reflection Questions – Progress, Not Perfection:

- At the end of each workday examine your actions for that day and assess if there was anything you had done that you wish you had not or if there were any decisions or actions you could have handled differently.

- Explain the purpose of completing a daily inventory and the necessity of making it a regular part of your work routine.

- Have you ever been disrespected at work in a way that caused you to react negatively? How did you feel and what did you do?

- Do you have difficulty admitting when you're wrong? If so, why do you think this is?

- How can promptly admitting your wrongs help you change your behavior?

- How does self-discipline apply to this step and why is it important?

- How does this step help you to live in the present?

- Have you ever had an employee admit that they had committed an error or failed to complete an assignment? How did you handle it? If approached again, how would you handle things differently?

STEP ELEVEN

We sought through introspection and contemplation to improve our understanding of the work we do and to discover the power to carry out this work to benefit others.

As a leader, your position of authority brings with it a certain level of responsibility. This can be a heavy weight to carry. Oftentimes, you may feel like no matter how hard you try, you are unable to obtain the goals you've established, whether it be for yourself, or more importantly, for your organization. During these times, it may be necessary to look inside yourself and examine your role and how it affects those with whom you work.

Commitment is the principle for this step. This concept is crucial because it requires you to regularly self-evaluate and determine the best means for you to improve the work you do. When done properly, you can gain many valuable insights.

When faced with problems at work, you may be at a loss for how to determine a solution. Or, at times, you may become frustrated or angry about push back from staff when you try to implement solutions.

One tool that can help you uncover the answers to your problems is meditation. You may have the misperception that meditation is all about chanting or trying to reach the astral plane. And for some, this is the purpose. Meditation, however, can be practiced in a very simple and pragmatic manner.

The first thing to understand is that meditation is not necessarily about emptying your mind. If anything, this can be virtually impossible. One method that you may want to try is the following:

sit comfortably with your eyes closed, or looking down, and breathe slowly, in and out to a count of three. While breathing, think of a problem you're encountering in your work. Allow yourself to examine the problem objectively. Then let it go. After doing so, simply relax and allow any impressions or thoughts that come to your mind to bubble up to the surface. Don't try to force an answer. Just let it come naturally. After practicing this method, you may begin to have a realization of the answer to your query.

Actually, meditation was how I came upon the idea to write this book. I was thinking about how I, a relatively new entrepreneur, could gain exposure and broaden my network. This is something that many people, like myself, have asked themselves. I used the technique I mentioned above and amazingly the idea of the book came to me. I realized that I could use my personal experience of being in long-term recovery and translate the spiritual principles found in the original 12 Steps into guiding principles that could be used in leadership.

Of course, it may not always be this simple, however if you practice this routine regularly you may find success. It's amazing what you can do if you open up your mind to this creative problem-solving process.

Step Eleven Reflection Questions – Looking Within:

- Have you ever felt angry, frustrated, or overwhelmed by a situation or problem you couldn't solve? Give an example and explain how you responded.

- How would you describe your relationship with your staff or colleagues?

- Have you had difficulty achieving goals at work? What have been the stumbling blocks?

- Do you meditate? If so, describe your method. If not, are you willing to try?

- How much time are you willing to set aside to meditate?

- Are you an "out of the box" thinker when it comes to solving problems? If so, describe a time when you came up with a creative idea to address an issue at work.

STEP TWELVE

Having had an awakening of spirit as a result of these steps, we tried to carry this message to others in our work and to practice these principles in all our affairs.

You've now come to the culmination of your journey of self-discovery. So, what do you do with what you've learned? For some of you, you may have had several "a-ha" moments as you've gone through this process. For others, it may be more subtle. But hopefully, you've noticed a change.

As a leader, it's important to be a good example to others. The concept of "servant leader" is what comes to mind when I think of the true definition of leadership. In your role as an executive or middle manager, think about the ways you've modeled the behaviors you expect others to follow. When doing so, it is important, yet again, to aim for objectivity.

The principles behind this step are unconditional love and selflessness. Believe it or not, when you practice unconditional love, you can be more forgiving of others, not to mention more able to recognize their mistakes. By doing so you can acknowledge the humanness found in everyone. Remember, none of us is perfect. Not you. Not me.

The principle of selflessness is paramount in this step because when operating from the perspective of a servant leader, you put the needs of others ahead of your own. This doesn't mean that you allow others to take advantage of you; It means that you are willing to sacrifice your potential "what's in it for me" attitude. Remember, it's about how you can incorporate what you've learned to benefit your organization.

If you've thoroughly worked the previous eleven steps, undoubtedly, you've learned some things about yourself you may have never realized. In this journey you can also take what you've learned to help others. One of the most fulfilling purposes a person can have is assisting others. In NA we say, "We can only keep what we have by giving it away." I know that by sharing my knowledge and experience with those with whom I work I am able to contribute to their growth and have a feeling of gratitude for having done so. This is done unconditionally, without expecting anything in return.

When you practice selfless service, you are able to demonstrate through not only your words, but your actions what it means to be a great leader. Think about those in your career who have had these qualities. We should all aspire to this kind of greatness. It's a matter of recognizing that you have the potential to be the same, in your own way.

This is not the end of the road. When you've completed working on this step you can cycle back at a later date and begin the process again, if you so choose. It's like peeling the layers off of an onion. You just keep getting closer to the core as you go forward. You've only just begun!

Step Twelve Reflection Questions – Being a Servant Leader:

- What has been your experience in going through the exercise of the 12 Steps?

- How have you changed? Do you believe these changes are long-lasting?

- How do you plan to "carry the message" to those at your organization?

- Give an example of when you showed unconditional love to one of your staff.

- Are you a servant leader? If so, how do you demonstrate this at work? If not, how can you model this behavior moving forward?

- Have you had any difficulty practicing any of the leadership principles explained in this guide? What were they and how do you plan to improve in these areas?

AFTERWORD

If you've taken the time to do the work presented here, you will gain valuable insights into who you are and what kind of leader you've become. Don't be dismayed if you have uncovered parts of yourself that need improving. As we have learned together, none of us is perfect. But it doesn't mean that you can't improve. This is hard work and it can take years to get to the place you're intended to be. That's okay. No one says you have to do this overnight. Take your time. The more thorough you've been, the better the results you will see.

I hope this has been beneficial to you. I know that if you've been willing to complete this exercise in a serious fashion then you're already on your way. And for that I congratulate you.

I wish you success in your endeavors!

Be well!

Made in the USA
Middletown, DE
09 September 2020